P9-DOC-692

Pinto Horses

ABDO
Publishing Company

A Buddy Book
by
Julie Murray

Published by Buddy Books, an imprint of ABDO Publishing Company, 4940 Viking Drive, Suite 622, Edina, Minnesota 55435. Copyright © 2005 by Abdo Consulting Group, Inc. International copyrights reserved in all countries. No part of this book may be reproduced in any form without written permission from the publisher.

Printed in the United States.

Edited by: Christy DeVillier
Contributing Editors: Matt Ray, Michael P. Goecke
Graphic Design: Maria Hosley
Image Research: Deborah Coldiron
Photographs: Corbis, Corel, Photodisc

Library of Congress Cataloging-in-Publication Data

Murray, Julie, 1969-
    Pinto horses/Julie Murray.
        p. cm. — (Animal kingdom Set II)
    Includes bibliographical references and index.
    Contents: Horses — Pinto horses — Color patterns — A horse's body — How they move — Feeding — Care of horses — Babies.
    ISBN 1-59197-331-7
        1. Pinto horse—Juvenile literature. [1. Pinto horse. 2. Horses.] I. Title.

SF293.P5M87 2003
636.1'3—dc21

                                                            2003044310

Contents

Horses

People tamed horses about 5,000 years ago. Today there are about 150 **breeds** of horses. The three main horse groups are coldbloods, hotbloods, and warmbloods.

The coldblood breeds are big horses. They are good workhorses. Clydesdales and Percherons are coldbloods.

There are many breeds of horses.

Hotblood **breeds** are slender and graceful horses. Thoroughbreds and Arabian horses are hotbloods.

Warmblood breeds are good at sporting. The American quarter horse is a warmblood breed.

This Arabian horse is a hotblood breed.

Ponies

Ponies are the smallest horses. Most adult ponies are less than 58 inches (147 cm) tall. Some ponies have pinto coloring.

One common pony **breed** is the Shetland pony. They are common as pets for children.

Pinto Horses

Long ago, Spanish explorers brought pinto horses to North America. Pinto horses were common among American Indians. Cowboys of the Wild West rode pintos, too.

The word *pinto* comes from the Spanish word *pintado*. It means "painted." Pinto horses have special colors and markings.

Many American Indians owned pinto horses.

Do pinto horses belong to one **breed**? The Pinto Association of America believes they do. But most countries do not place pintos into a breed group.

Size And Body

Pinto horses can be different sizes. Some people measure horses in **hands**. One hand equals four inches (ten cm). Most pintos grow to become between 14 and 16 hands. That is about five feet (two m) tall.

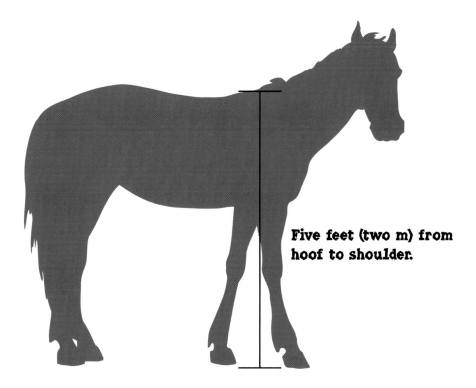

Five feet (two m) from hoof to shoulder.

Horses have a long head. The long hair on a horse's neck and back is its **mane**. Horses move around on strong, thin legs. On their feet are hard coverings called **hooves**.

Pinto Coloring

A pinto's coloring sets it apart from other horses. Pintos have a base color with patches of another color. White, black, tan, brown, gray, and reddish are common coat colors.

This pinto has tobiano coloring.

There are two types of coloring for pintos. One color type is called tobiano. Tobiano pintos have a white base color with patches of another color.

The other color type is called overo. Overo pintos have white patches on a different base color.

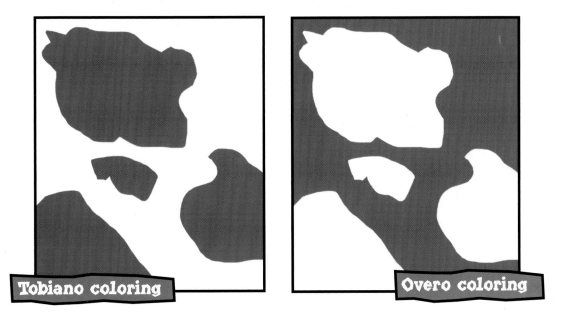

Tobiano coloring

Overo coloring

This pinto horse
has overo coloring.

How They Move

The way a horse moves is its **gait**. Horses have four gaits. They can walk, trot, canter, or gallop. Walking is the slowest gait. Galloping is the fastest gait.

A trotting gait is faster than a walking gait. A trotting horse goes about nine miles (14 km) per hour.

A canter is faster than a trot. A cantering horse goes as fast as 12 miles (19 km) per hour.

Eating

Horses eat grass, hay, oats, and bran. Adults need about 20 pounds (nine kg) of food every day. Horses need water every day, too. They can drink about 12 gallons (45 l) of water each day.

A horse's front teeth have sharp edges. They use their front teeth for biting. Horses use their back teeth for chewing.

Care

Horses have a lot of needs. They need fresh food and water every day. They need a large space for exercising. Horses also need a clean shelter called a stall.

Owners should brush and comb their horses. Brushing helps to keep them clean.

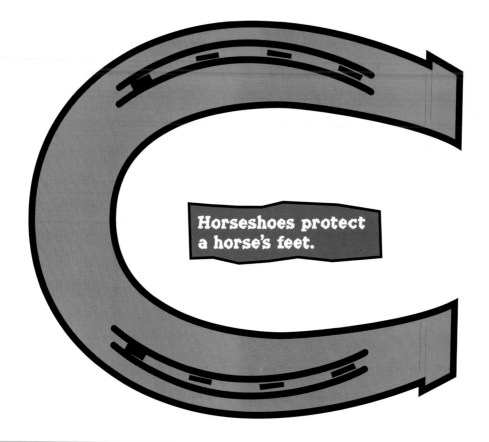

Horseshoes protect a horse's feet.

Taking care of a horse's **hooves** is very important. Owners should trim and clean their horse's hooves. Some owners put horseshoes on their horses. Horseshoes help to protect their feet.

Foals

Female horses, or **mares**, can have a baby once a year. A baby horse is called a **foal**. Wild mares mostly have their foals in the spring.

A mare with her foal.

Newborn **foals** can stand within minutes. They drink their mother's milk for about six months. Six-week-old foals will begin to eat other food. Horses become adults after three or four years. Horses may live as long as 25 years.

Pinto horses are beautiful animals.

Important Words

breed a special group of horses. Horses of the same breed look alike and share certain characteristics.

foal a young horse less than one year old.

gait the way a horse moves.

hand something used to measure horses. One hand equals four inches (ten cm).

hooves the special horn-covering on the feet of some animals.

mane the long hair that grows on a horse's neck and back.

mare a female horse.

Web Sites

To learn more about pinto horses, visit ABDO Publishing Company on the World Wide Web. Web sites about pinto horses are featured on our Book Links page. These links are routinely monitored and updated to provide the most current information available.

www.abdopub.com

Index